ROBERT SCHUMANN

ADVICE TO YOUNG MUSICIANS

MUSICAL RULES FOR HOME AND IN LIFE

Introduction & Biography © 2010 by Barbara Allman

Book Design by Michelle Ste. Marie

Illustrations © 2010 JupiterImages Corporation

Published by

Raro Press
179 Niblick Road, #134
Paso Robles, CA 93446
www.raropress.com

ISBN: 978-0-615-35858-1

"The artist's vocation—to send light into the depths of the human heart."

ROBERT SCHUMANN

This edition of *Advice to Young Musicians: Musical Rules for Home and in Life* commemorates the 200th anniversary of the birth of composer Robert Schumann, born June 8, 1810, in Zwickau, Germany.

In 1848, Schumann wrote a collection of keyboard pieces intended for young music students. It was the year his eldest child, Marie, turned seven. In a letter to a friend, he described his Album for the Young op. 68: "These pieces became especially dear to my heart, and they are taken right out of family life. I wrote the first pieces in the Album especially for our oldest child on her birthday, and the rest just came one after another."

Schumann's manuscript included words of musical advice as well. However, the *Musical Rules for Home and in Life* did not appear in print until a later edition of the Album. Originally written in German, this version is based on the 1860 English translation by Henry Hugo Pierson and uses some wording more easily accessible to modern readers, young and old.

Countless piano students have enjoyed the task of learning Schumann's delightful piano pieces— ("Melody," "The Happy Farmer") —but fewer are familiar with the wisdom passed on in this little book of advice—some of it practical, some humorous, and some profound. It is an uncommon offering from a remarkable composer who shares both his musical and literary gifts with the ages.

Raro Press
December, 2009

ROBERT SCHUMANN

"Ländliches Lied," from No. 20, Album for the Young.

ADVICE TO YOUNG MUSICIANS

MUSICAL RULES FOR HOME AND IN LIFE

BY
ROBERT SCHUMANN
1848

ROBERT SCHUMANN

The cultivation of the ear is of the greatest importance. Endeavor early to recognize each tone and key. Find out the exact notes sounded by the bell, the glass, the cuckoo, etc.

Practice frequently the scales and other finger exercises; but this alone is not sufficient. There are many people who think to obtain grand results in this way, and who up to a mature age spend many hours daily in mechanical labor. That is about the same as if we tried every day to pronounce the alphabet with greater fluency! You can employ your time more usefully.

There are such things as "silent keyboards." Try them for awhile, and you will discover that they are useless. The silent cannot teach us to speak.

Play strictly in time! The playing of many a virtuoso resembles the walk of an intoxicated person. Do not take such as your example.

Learn early on the fundamental principles of harmony.

Do not be afraid of the words *theory*,
thoroughbass, counterpoint, etc.
You will understand their full meaning
in due time.

Never jingle! Always play with energy
and do not leave a piece unfinished.

You may play too slowly or too fast;
both are faults.

Endeavor to play easy pieces well and
with elegance; that is better than to
play difficult pieces badly.

ROBERT SCHUMANN

Take care always to have your instrument well tuned.

It is not only necessary that you should be able to play your pieces on the instrument, but you should also be able to hum the air without the piano.

Strengthen your imagination so that you may not only recall the melody of a composition, but even the harmony that belongs to it.

Even with a poor voice, endeavor to
sing at first sight without the aid of
the instrument; by doing so your ear
for music will constantly improve.
But in case you are endowed with a
good voice, do not hesitate a moment
to cultivate it. Consider it the most
valuable gift heaven has granted you!

You must reach the point where you
are able to understand a piece of music
upon paper.

When you play, never mind who
listens to you.

ROBERT SCHUMANN

Always play as if in the presence of a master.

If anyone should place before you a composition to play at sight, read it over before you play it.

When you have done your musical day's work and feel tired, do not exert yourself further. It is better to rest than to work without pleasure and enthusiasm.

When you grow older, do not play what is purely fashionable. Time is precious. One would need to live a hundred lives to become acquainted with all the good works that exist.

Children cannot be brought up
in sound health if they are fed
sweetmeats, pastry, and candy.
The mental food must be as simple
and nourishing as the bodily. Great
composers have sufficiently provided
for the former; keep to their works.

All bravura music soon grows
antiquated. Technical feats are
valuable only when used to perfect
the performance of real music.

Never help to circulate bad
compositions; on the contrary, help
to suppress them with earnestness.

ROBERT SCHUMANN

You should neither play bad
compositions, nor listen to them,
unless you are forced to.

Do not think velocity, or passage-
playing, your highest aim. Try to
produce such an impression with
a piece of music as was intended
by the composer; anything further
is caricature.

Think it vile to alter works of good
composers, to omit parts of them,
or to insert new-fashioned ornaments.
This is the greatest insult you can
offer to Art.

In choosing which pieces to study,
ask the advice of more experienced
persons than yourself; by so doing, you
will save much time.

You must gradually become
acquainted with all the principal
works of the great masters.

Do not be elated by the applause of
the masses. The approval of artists is
of greater value to you.

ROBERT SCHUMANN

All that is merely fashionable will go out of fashion, and if you keep on with it until you grow up, you will appear a fop whom nobody respects.

Much playing in society is more injurious than useful. Suit the taste and capacity of your audience; but never play anything which deep down you know is trashy and worthless.

Do not miss an opportunity of practicing music in company with other musicians; as for example in duets, trios, etc. This gives you a flowing and elevated style of playing, and self-possession. Frequently accompany singers.

If all would play first violin, we could not have an orchestra. Therefore respect every musician in his own place.

Love your particular instrument, but be not vain enough to consider it the greatest and only one. Remember that there are others as fine as yours. Remember also that singers exist, and that numbers, both in chorus and orchestra, produce the most sublime music; therefore do not overrate the solo.

ROBERT SCHUMANN

As you grow up, associate more with scores than with virtuosos.

Frequently play the fugues of good masters, above all, those by Johann Sebastian Bach. Let his "Well-Tempered Clavier" be your daily bread. By these means you will certainly become a proficient musician.

Let your closest friends be those who are better informed than yourself.

Relieve the severity of your musical studies by reading poetry. Take many a walk in the fields and woods!

Johann Sebastian Bach

24   ROBERT SCHUMANN

You may learn much from vocalists,
but do not believe all that they say.

Remember, there are more people in
the world than yourself. Be modest!
You have not yet invented nor thought
anything that others have not thought
or invented before. And if you should
have an original thought, consider it
a gift from heaven, which you are to
share with others.

By studying the history of music, and
by hearing the masterpieces that have
been produced at different periods, you
will be most readily cured of vanity or
presumption.

A book that you will find valuable to read is: *On Purity in Music*, by Thibaut, a German professor. Read it often, when you have matured.

If you pass a church and hear an organ, go in and listen. If allowed to sit on the organ bench, try your inexperienced fingers and marvel at the supreme power of music.

Do not miss an opportunity of practicing on the organ. There is no instrument that can so effectually correct errors or impurity of style and touch as that one.

ROBERT SCHUMANN

Frequently sing in choirs, especially the middle parts. This will help to make you a real musician.

ROBERT SCHUMANN

What does it mean to be *musical* ?
You are not musical if your eyes are fixed on
the notes with anxiety and you labor through
a piece. You are not musical if, (supposing
that somebody should turn over two pages at
once) you stop short and cannot proceed. But
you are musical if you can almost foresee in a
new piece what is to follow, or remember it in
an old one—in a word, if you have not only
music in your fingers, but also in your head
and heart.

But how do we become musical?
This, my young friend, is a gift from above;
it consists chiefly of a fine ear and quick
perception. And these gifts may be cultivated
and enhanced. You will not become musical
by confining yourself to your room and to
working on mere mechanical studies, but by
taking part in the musical world, especially
with the chorus and the orchestra.

Become acquainted early on with the range of the human voice in its four parts. Pay attention to it especially in the chorus, examine in what tones its highest power lies, in what others it can be employed to affect the soft and tender passions.

Pay attention to national airs and folksongs; they contain a treasure trove of the finest melodies, and open to you a glimpse of the character of the different nations.

Fail not to practice the reading of old clefs, otherwise many treasures of past times will remain a closed fountain to you.

Attend early to the tone and character
of the various instruments; try to impress
their particular sound on your ear.

Do not neglect to attend good operas.

Highly esteem the old, but take also
a warm interest in the new. Be not
prejudiced against names unknown
to you.

ROBERT SCHUMANN

Do not judge a composition from the first time hearing it; that which pleases you at first is not always the best. Masters need to be studied. Many things will not become clear to you till you have reached a more advanced age.

When judging compositions, discriminate between works of real art and those merely meant to amuse amateurs. Cherish the former, and do not get angry with the others.

"Melody" is the battle-cry of amateurs, and certainly music without melody is nothing. Understand, however, what these persons mean by melody: a simple, flowing and pleasing rhythmical tune; this is enough to satisfy them. There are, however, others of a different sort, and whenever you open Bach, Mozart, Beethoven, or any real master, their melodies meet you in a thousand different shapes. I trust you will soon be tired of the inferior melodies, especially those out of the latest Italian operas.

If you attempt to form little melodies
while at the piano, that is very well;
but if they come into your mind
of themselves, when you are not
practicing, you can be even more
pleased; for an inner sense of music is
then stirring in you. The fingers must
do what the head desires; not the other
way around.

If you begin to compose, work it out
in your head. Do not try a piece on
your instrument until you have fully
conceived it. If your music came from
your heart and soul, and you felt it
yourself, it will affect others in the
same manner.

If heaven has bestowed on you a fine imagination, you will often be seated at your piano in solitary hours, as if attached to it. You will desire to express the feelings of your heart in harmony, and the more clouded the sphere of harmony may perhaps be to you, the more mysteriously you will feel as if drawn into magic circles.

In youth these may be your happiest hours. Beware, however, of abandoning yourself too often to the influence of a talent that induces you to lavish powers and time, as it were, upon phantoms. Mastery over the forms of composition and a clear expression of your ideas can only be attained by constant writing. Write, therefore, more than you improvise.

Acquire early a knowledge of the art
of conducting music. Observe the best
conductors, and conduct along with
them in your mind. This will give
you clearness of perception and make
you accurate.

Look deeply into life, and study it as
diligently as the other arts and sciences.

The laws of morality are also
those of Art.

By means of hard work and
perseverance you will rise higher
and higher.

From a pound of iron, that costs little,
a thousand watch-springs can be made,
whose value becomes prodigious. Use
faithfully the pound you have received
from the Lord.

Without enthusiasm nothing great can
be accomplished in art.

The object of art is not to produce
riches. Become a great artist, and all
other desirable accessories will fall to
your lot.

The spirit will not become clear to you, until you understand the form.

Perhaps genius alone understands genius fully.

It has been said that a perfect musician must be able to see, in his mind's eye, any new, and even complicated, piece of orchestral music as if in full score lying before him! This is indeed the greatest triumph of musical intellect that can be imagined.

There is no end to learning.

ROBERT SCHUMANN

THE LIFE OF ROBERT SCHUMANN

Robert Schumann
June 8, 1810 – July 29, 1856

Robert Schumann was a German
Romantic composer and influential
music critic, born in Zwickau,
Saxony. His father was a publisher
and bookseller, from whom Robert
inherited his literary leanings. Robert
displayed extraordinary musical talent
at a very young age, improvising and
composing at the grand piano his
father bought for him.

His father died when Robert was
sixteen, and in 1828 his determined
mother insisted on sending him to law
school at the University of Leipzig to
prepare for a profession. Schumann
preferred studying music and poetry,
and begged his mother to allow him to
follow his heart. At twenty, he became
a pupil of Friedrich Wieck, who was
known for his piano teaching. Wieck
had been instructing his own young
daughter, Clara, who was a musical
prodigy and an accomplished concert
pianist from the age of nine.

After injuring his hand, probably
with a device meant to stretch the
fingers for playing, Schumann
turned to composing music instead
of performing. On his own, he
made a study of the works of Bach.
Later, he studied composition with
composer and conductor Heinrich
Dorn, who recognized Schumann's

gifts and encouraged him to pursue a nontraditional course of compositional studies.

By age twenty-three, Schumann was composing works that were fresh, new, and different from other music of the time. Already a complete romantic, he wrote: "I believe music to be the ideal language of the soul: some think it is only intended to tickle the ear, while others treat it like a mathematical calculation."

With a group of friends, Schumann founded an avant-garde music journal—*Neue Zeitschrift für Musik.* He became its editor at twenty-four and remained in that capacity for ten years. His informed, intelligent writing style was influential in encouraging his readership to appreciate the new and noteworthy.

He had strong views as a critic, and was frequently generous in his praise of other worthy composers. Through the years, Robert championed the music of Mendelssohn, Chopin, and Brahms, among others. He used the pseudonyms *Florestan* and *Eusebius* in his writing—Florestan if the tone were fiery and passionate, and Eusebius for his dreamy, poetic musings. Sometimes a third voice, *Master Raro*, injected a balanced viewpoint into the imaginary conversations Schumann created. The journal was only one side of his creative output, however, as he continued his own exceptional compositional work.

Robert grew to love Clara Wieck as she matured, but her father vehemently opposed their relationship. He attempted to thwart their engagement both privately and publicly in the legal courts. He may have felt his long efforts at shaping his daughter into a musical virtuoso would no longer yield him a lucrative income if Clara married.

Clara Wieck

As a young woman, Clara was a force
to be reckoned with in the concert
world, winning imperial accolades and
wild popularity in Germany, France,
Denmark, England and Russia. (She
would remain a premier performer
into old age.)

The young couple defied Friedrich Wieck and won the legal right to marry. In the turbulent year before they married, Robert composed more than a hundred beautiful art songs in his own fresh style. On September 12, 1840, one day before Clara's twenty-first birthday, they were wed.

Clara and Robert Schumann

Robert continued to compose throughout their sixteen-year marriage, working his way through every form: works for piano and orchestra, for piano and voice, opera, chorale, chamber music, and four symphonies. Clara continued to concertize and promoted his works in her performances. She also gave birth to their eight children: Marie, Elise, Julie, Emil, Ludwig, Ferdinand, Eugenie, and Felix.

Schumann struggled with mental illness at the end of his life. When he realized his illness had overtaken him, he requested to be confined to an asylum, where he died a year and a half later. His works have secured him a place of honor in the pantheon of important Romantic composers.